Newbridge Discovery Links®

America the Beautiful

Cynthia Rothman

Newbridge

America the Beautiful
ISBN: 978-1-4007-3655-3

Program Author: Dr. Brenda Parkes, Literacy Expert

Written by Cynthia Rothman
Design assistance by Kirchoff/Wohlberg, Inc.

Newbridge Publishing, LLC
33 Boston Post Road West, Suite 440, Marlborough, MA 01752

Cover Photograph: Grand Teton National Park, Wyoming
Table of Contents Photograph: Monument Valley, Arizona

Photo Credits
Cover: Greg Martin/SuperStock; Table of Contents page: SuperStock; page 4: Bob Thomason/Getty Images;
page 5: (top) from *Hymns and Sacred Songs*, Edited By E.O. Excell. Chicago: Hope, 1918. Courtesy University
of Colorado at Boulder, Music Library, (bottom) AP/Wide World Photos; page 8: Jim Roetzel/Dembinsky
Photo Associates; page 9: Brian Miller/Bruce Coleman, Inc.; page 10: Michael Melford/Getty Images; page
11: Bruce Dale/National Geographic; page 12: F. Schussler/Getty Images; page 13: John Blaustein/Woodfin
Camp & Associates; page 14: Kevin Horan/Getty Images; page 15: (left) AP/Wide World Photos, (right)
Mark J. Thomas/Dembinsky Photo Associates; page 16: Chris Sanders/Getty Images; page 17: (left) Carl R.
Sams II/Dembinsky Photo Associates, (right) Ken Scott/Dembinsky Photo Associates, (inset) Ken Scott/
Dembinsky Photo Associates; page 18: Mark E. Gibson/Dembinsky Photo Associates; page 19: (top) Joseph
Sohm/Photo Researchers, (center) Joseph Sohm/Photo Researchers, (bottom) Mark E. Gibson/Dembinsky
Photo Associates; page 20: Brian Yarvin/Photo Researchers; page 21: (top) David Muench/Getty Images,
(bottom) Phil Degginger/Bruce Coleman, Inc.; page 22: Jamie Squire/Getty Images

Map by Michael DiGiorgio, pages 6-7

Printed by Nordica International Ltd.
Manufactured in Guangzhou, China
April, 2010
Nordica Job#: 03-104-10
Sundance/Newbridge PO#: 510208

Table of Contents

America's Song

Katherine Lee Bates visited Pikes Peak, Colorado, in 1893. Located in Pike National Forest, Pikes Peak is 14,109 feet high. Today, hikers still enjoy climbing Pikes Peak.

The view was breathtaking when Katherine Lee Bates stood looking out from Pikes Peak in Colorado. She had traveled across America and was amazed by its magnificent sights.

When she returned home to Massachusetts, she wrote a poem she called "America the Beautiful." In her poem, she told about what she had seen. Years later the poem became a song set to music written by Samuel Ward.

More than a hundred years have passed since the writing of "America the Beautiful," but it is still a popular patriotic American song.

These children are learning "America the Beautiful" in sign language.

We can only imagine what Katherine Lee Bates saw as she traveled across America. But, here's a chance to take your own trip across the country and see beautiful America.

Fast Facts About the United States

- The United States covers 3,615,276 square miles and stretches from the Atlantic Ocean to the Pacific Ocean.

- Point Barrow, Alaska, is the northernmost point in the United States. Can you find the easternmost point in the United States?

- The Mississippi River and the Missouri River are the two longest rivers in the United States. Can you find where the Missouri flows into the Mississippi?

- There are four major mountain ranges in the United States—the Rocky Mountains, the Appalachian Mountains, the Sierra Nevada, and the Cascade Mountains.

- Coal, oil, and timber are just a few of the **natural resources** found in the United States.

Map Key
- City
- National capital
- Rivers
- Mountains

As you read, think about all the resources that make America such an amazing country.
This map shows the places you will visit.

The United States of America

The Rocky Mountains

Trees from Rocky Mountain forests are a natural resource. Trees are a **renewable resource** because when trees are cut down, new ones can be planted.

The majestic Rocky Mountains stretch across North America and run through six states— Montana, Idaho, Wyoming, Utah, Colorado, and New Mexico. The Rockies are the largest mountain chain in the United States.

The Rocky Mountains are full of natural resources. **Minerals** such as gold, silver, and **zinc** are mined there. Water and timber are other precious natural resources that come from these mountains.

The Rocky Mountains are a special part of our country. That's why our government created Rocky Mountain National Park in Colorado. The land in the park is protected. More than three million people visit Rocky Mountain National Park each year. Look around! You are surrounded by beauty. And you might see a black bear, a moose, or a bighorn sheep.

Many of our country's biggest rivers begin in the Rocky Mountains. When the winter snow melts on the mountaintops, it fills freshwater streams. Those streams carry water to rivers like the Colorado, the Missouri, and the Rio Grande.

The Great Plains

In one year, farmers in Kansas harvested 506 million bushels of wheat—that's enough wheat to make more than 36 billion loaves of bread.

Fields of ripe, yellow wheat blow in the wind across the Great Plains of the United States. The Great Plains is the large area of flat land in America's midwest. The region includes parts of North and South Dakota, Nebraska, Kansas, and Iowa.

This part of the country is called the breadbasket. Bread is made from **grain**, and most of the grain we eat is grown there. The flat, treeless land is just right for growing wheat and other grains.

Kansas and North Dakota grow more wheat than any other states. After wheat is harvested, it is ground into flour to make breads, cereals, and pasta. More than half of the wheat grown in Kansas is sent to other countries and sold there.

Corn is grown in Iowa and Nebraska. Most of the corn is used to feed cattle, sheep, and pigs, but some corn from the Great Plains is used in food for people.

Today, machines do much of the work of planting and harvesting, so farmers can grow large amounts of grain on huge farms. A farm machine called a **combine** can harvest an acre of wheat in less than six minutes.

Farmers on the Great Plains also grow oats, rye, and soybeans.

Thousands of things, from diapers to packing "peanuts," are made with corn products. Cornstarch is used to make paper and cardboard. Corn syrup is used to sweeten soda and other food.

California's Fields

California produces strawberries in its warm, coastal regions. Its warm sunny days and foggy nights are perfect for growing strawberries.

What do apples and plums, walnuts and lettuce, tomatoes and peaches all have in common? They are all grown in California. While most of our country's wheat and corn comes from the Great Plains states, California leads the country in the production of many fruits and vegetables. The **climate** in California is just right for growing these crops.

Grown in California

Ninety-one percent of the grapes grown in the United States are grown in California! What percentage of other fruits and vegetables grown in the United States are grown in California in an average year?

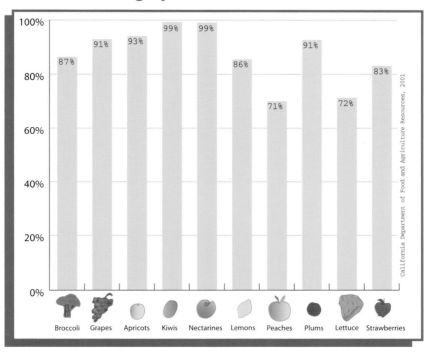

Chart values:
- Broccoli: 87%
- Grapes: 91%
- Apricots: 93%
- Kiwis: 99%
- Nectarines: 99%
- Lemons: 86%
- Peaches: 71%
- Plums: 91%
- Lettuce: 72%
- Strawberries: 83%

California Department of Food and Agriculture Resources, 2001

California's mild climate means that fruits and vegetables can be grown almost all year long. People in colder climates can eat fresh California fruits and vegetables during the winter.

The Mississippi River

Grain from farms across the Midwest is loaded onto barges along the Mississippi River and shipped to New Orleans, Louisiana. There, **cargo** is sent on freighters to countries around the world.

The "Mighty Mississippi" starts as a small stream, only about eight meters wide, near Lake Itasca, Minnesota. It grows larger as it flows south, and rivers and streams from both the east and west feed into it. In spots, it stretches to more than 900 meters wide. By the time it empties into the Gulf of Mexico, the Mississippi River has traveled more than 2,320 miles.

The Mississippi, which is the largest river in North America, is a major transportation route that has helped America grow. Throughout our country's history, people have used the Mississippi as a river road to move people and goods, such as grains and steel, from place to place. Long ago, traders traveled along the Mississippi and settled in towns on the river's banks. Later, steamships transported goods along the river. Today, cargo is still carried on the Mississippi River.

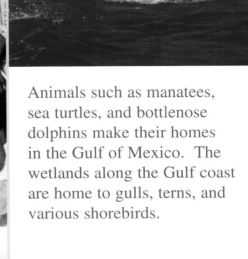

Animals such as manatees, sea turtles, and bottlenose dolphins make their homes in the Gulf of Mexico. The wetlands along the Gulf coast are home to gulls, terns, and various shorebirds.

The Great Lakes

Not salty like the ocean, the Great Lakes are a rich source of water. With the rivers and channels that connect them, these five lakes make up about one-fifth of Earth's surface **freshwater**.

Look at a map of the United States or a photo taken from space of North America. It's easy to spot the Great Lakes. Five lakes make up the Great Lakes—Lake Michigan, Lake Erie, Lake Superior, Lake Huron, and Lake Ontario. The Great Lakes are very large. If you stand on the shore of one of them, looking out over the water is like looking at the ocean.

Native Americans and early settlers from Europe used the Great Lakes as a roadway for exploring unknown lands. Later, towns and cities—including Chicago, Illinois; Gary, Indiana; and Toledo, Ohio—grew up around the Great Lakes.

Like the Mississippi River, the Great Lakes are still used for transportation. Through a series of rivers and canals, all five of the lakes are connected. The Saint Lawrence Seaway connects them to the Atlantic Ocean.

Iron mined in Wisconsin and Minnesota can be shipped to steel mills in Ohio. Coal can be shipped from the East to factories in the Midwest.

The land around the Great Lakes has rich soil. These are cherry orchards in Michigan, where most of the tart cherries used in pies, jams, and candies are grown.

Every year, thousands of tourists visit Michigan's Upper Peninsula, which is bordered by Lake Michigan, Lake Superior, and Lake Huron. There are places to swim, fish, and camp, and many beautiful sights to see.

17

Bustling Cities

Washington, D.C.
The Capitol building is where the Senate and House of Representatives meet to develop the laws that govern our nation.

America is full of natural wonders—from the Great Lakes and the Mississippi River to the fertile lands of the Great Plains and California. But America's cities are also wonders, full of exciting things to do and see.

The capital city of the United States is Washington, D.C. It is the center of the American government and is visited by people from around the world. The White House has been home to every president, except George Washington.

Los Angeles, California

Los Angeles is the second largest city in the United States. Throughout its history it has been the most important port city on the West Coast. Los Angeles is also home to the film industry, which started there.

Chicago, Illinois

Chicago overlooks Lake Michigan and is the only city that links the Great Lakes with the Mississippi River. Through its history it had been an important port city and still is today. Chicago is known for its skyscrapers, and its skyline is dotted with hotels and office buildings.

Houston, Texas

Houston is located about 50 miles from the Gulf of Mexico. The Port of Houston is the second largest port in the country. Oil was discovered near Houston in 1901, and today Houston is a center for the oil industry. Houston is also the home of NASA's Johnson Space Center.

America's Wonders

Niagara Falls State Park is the oldest state park in America. It was created to keep the land around the Niagara River and the falls protected and open to visitors.

A **waterfall** forms when a river falls over a cliff. As the Niagara River flows from Lake Erie to Lake Ontario, it forms one of the most spectacular waterfalls in the world—Niagara Falls. Niagara Falls is actually made up of two big waterfalls. Horseshoe Falls is about 670 meters wide and 56 meters high. The American Falls is about 323 meters wide and 57 meters high.

Niagara Falls is located on the border of the United States and Canada. Horseshoe Falls is in Canada, and the American Falls is in the United States.

Niagara Falls is not the only natural wonder you can see while traveling through the United States.

The Grand Canyon in Arizona is one of the deepest and biggest **canyons** in the world. One mile deep, the Grand Canyon was carved out over millions and millions of years by the Colorado River.

The Hawaiian Islands were formed by volcanoes. One of the world's most active **volcanoes**, Kilauea, is on the island of Hawaii.

From Sea to Shining Sea!

The song "America the Beautiful" ends with the words "From sea to shining sea." America is a vast land that stretches from the Atlantic Ocean to the Pacific Ocean.

America has many riches and resources. It has great cities and rich farmlands. It has huge mountain ranges that seem to go on forever and rivers and lakes that sparkle with freshwater.

The people who live in America are a precious resource, too. Americans are proud of their freedom. And they are proud of this beautiful country.

Glossary

canyon: a deep valley with steep sides

cargo: goods or materials carried or moved by boat, train, truck, or plane

climate: the average course of weather in a place

combine: a machine used by farmers to harvest grain

freshwater: water that does not contain salt and can be used for drinking

grain: the edible seeds of certain plants. Oats, rice, barley, and wheat are grains.

mineral: a natural substance that we usually get out of the ground, such as gold, salt, and oil

natural resource: a useful material found in nature, such as wood, oil, or silver

renewable resource: a resource that is able to be replaced in nature

waterfall: a steep fall of water, usually formed when a river flows over a cliff

volcano: a mountain formed by eruptions of rock from the earth's core. Volcanoes can form on the ocean floor.

zinc: a blue-white metal found in the earth; used to coat metal objects and prevent rust

Index

Websites

Learn more about the United States by visiting:

www.americaslibrary.gov/cgi-bin/page.cgi
www.enchantedlearning.com/usa/states/